# Your Child at 5

Working at home with your child can be a very enjo[yable] shared experience. It is also an invaluable part of his education.

This book gives a selection of activities which most 5-yea[r] olds should be able to perform and enjoy. It is for children in the Reception Year about to start work on the National Curriculum.

All the activities are closely linked to the National Curriculum and practise important skills in the three core subjects, Mathematics, English and Science. The Notes for Parents on pages 2-3 include simple symbols to show which subject skills are practised in each activity.

M Maths E English S Science

You can help your child to get the best out of this book by:

- finding a quiet time when you are both relaxed and undisturbed. Enjoy the time together and the activity.
- letting your child help select an activity.
- talking about each activity, exchanging opinions, working out problems. This develops your child's speaking and listening skills which will help all other areas of learning.
- trying to finish on a positive point, before your child gets tired. Let him or her control the pace.
- always giving plenty of praise and encouragement. Everyone responds well if they feel they are succeeding.

Rhona Whiteford and Jim Fitzsimmons
Illustrated by Peter Kavanagh

Headway • Hodder & Stoughton

# NOTES FOR PARENTS

**Pages 4-5 Ten minute traffic survey** M

Discuss the page together, then spend a ten minute period counting the vehicles that pass your house. This activity practises handling data and using maths in a practical situation.

**Page 6 Busy bathtime** M

Use this page to help your child get a basic understanding of capacity.

**Page 7 Measuring** M

By using household objects as units of measurement, your child will begin to see that a standard unit is needed for comparison of size. Make sure the items are placed alongside each other, with no spaces in-between.

**Pages 8-9 Underwater counting** M

Counting from 1 to 10. Encourage your child to point to each item in the set.

**Page 10 What time is it?** M

Use a toy clock or an old one, to show how the big hand points up to twelve and the small hand points to the hour number when it is o'clock. Talk about the different times of day when you do particular things such as eat, go shopping, or go to bed. Round up times to the nearest hour to avoid confusion.

**Page 11 Smarty party** M

More practice in matching number and quantity, with the added advantage of being able to eat the answers.

**Page 12 Pirate treasure** M

By colouring the same number of beads on the necklace as the number on the end, a pattern will emerge to show all the number bonds to ten. You can get the same effect by using an abacus.

**Page 13 Dotty castle** E

This is a tracking exercise that introduces the basics of letter formation. If the whole picture is too daunting a task, let your child complete one section at a time.

**Pages 14-15 Toy shop** E

This is to help your child recognise the letter sounds of the alphabet. When looking at the pictures around the edge, say the sound of the letter, for example 'a' as in apple.

**Pages 16-17 Writing** E

Use this page to practise left-to-right tracking, and as an introduction to the formation of the letters 'o, a, c, d, g, q'.

**Page 18 Reading together** E

Read with your child and look at the pictures in the text to try to guess the missing word. Look at the word bank at the bottom of the page to choose the most suitable one. Discuss what 'Dad' changed into.

**Page 19 Feelings** E

Talk about the kind of things which make people feel happy, sad, angry or frightened. Write down the list of things to help promote discussion and widen vocabulary.

**Page 20 Spellings** E

Get your child to look at the picture and say the word, then look at the letter bank and select a letter to complete the word.

**Page 21 A word think tank** E

Talk about water with your child and think of as many different words as you can to describe it. Write them down in the splashes. The collection of words will help to develop vocabulary and imagination, and can be used to help write or tell a story.

**Page 22 Right word** E

Talk about the picture together. Read out the beginning of the sentences and then ask your child to choose the most suitable endings. This sort of exercise helps develop listening skills, understanding and observation.

**Page 23 Dinosaur World** S E

This activity explores living and non-living things, and shows how to create a small self-sufficient environment, just like our earth.

**Page 24 Build a car** S E

A simple, practical challenge in problem solving using a popular toy. Explain to your child that the chassis is the base-frame of a car.

**Page 25 A kaleidoscope** S E

By following instructions you can make a fun toy and explore the properties of light and reflection. Make sure your child uses special safety scissors.

**Pages 26-27 Shadows** S E

This gives further opportunities to explore the properties of light and the formation of shadows. Look at the length of shadows at different times of the day and discuss the reasons for this.

**Pages 28-29 Home from school** S E

This is a fun game to help promote awareness of the environment and personal safety.

**Page 30 Static electricity** S E

This is a simple exploration of producing low-power electricity, followed by an investigation of the kinds of materials affected by it, and the way in which certain materials react.

**Page 31 All about me** S E

Use this sheet to help develop self-awareness and focus on the personal characteristics of your child.

# Traffic survey

Go outside and stand in a safe place or look through the window. Count how much traffic goes past your house in ten minutes. Use a crayon to colour or tick a box each time you see any of these vehicles.

| | | | | | | | | | | | |
|---|---|---|---|---|---|---|---|---|---|---|---|
|  bus | | | | | | | | | | | altogether |
| | | | | | | | | | | | |
| | | | | | | | | | | | |
| | | | | | | | | | | | |

| | | | | | | | | | | | |
|---|---|---|---|---|---|---|---|---|---|---|---|
|  car | | | | | | | | | | | altogether |
| | | | | | | | | | | | |
| | | | | | | | | | | | |
| | | | | | | | | | | | |

| | | | | | | | | | | | |
|---|---|---|---|---|---|---|---|---|---|---|---|
|  lorry | | | | | | | | | | | altogether |
| | | | | | | | | | | | |
| | | | | | | | | | | | |
| | | | | | | | | | | | |

Do this survey at different times of the day to see when the road is busiest.

van

altogether

bicycle

altogether

tanker

altogether

emergency vehicles

altogether

Which vehicle did you see most of?

I saw most ______________________

# Busy bathtime

Take a plastic cup , a plastic squeezy bottle  and a bowl.

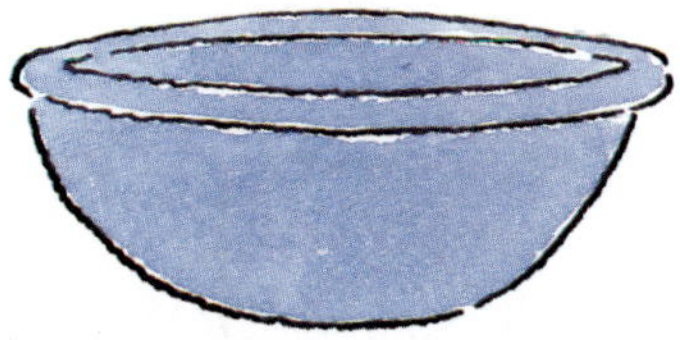

Guess how many cups and bottles of water you will need to fill the bowl. Write the number in the 'Guess' box. Then try it out in the bath and fill in the 'Actual' box.

How many  of water to fill the bowl?

Guess ☐ Actual ☐

How many  of water to fill the bowl?

Guess ☐ Actual ☐

# Measuring

Use these things to measure objects from around your house. Then fill in the boxes below.

My chair is ☐ cans high.

Our table is ☐ straws long.

My favourite book is ☐ blocks long.

My shoe is ☐ matchboxes long.

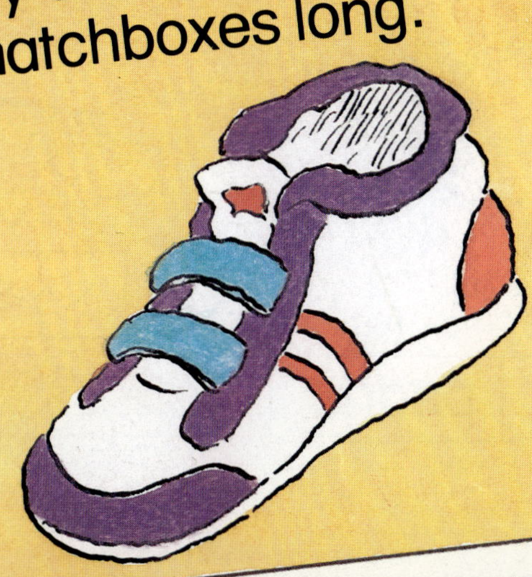

# Underwater counting

Can you count all these things and write the numbers in the boxes?

sharks
jellyfish
eels
starfish
crabs

# What time is it?

Draw the hands on the clocks and write in the times.

breakfast time | 8 | o'clock

lunch time | 12 | o'clock

tea/dinner time | 5 | o'clock

bedtime | 8 | o'clock

Draw yourself at your favourite time of the day!

# Smarty party

Use raisins or small sweets to complete these pictures. Write how many you used in the boxes.

# Pirate treasure

Look at the numbers on each necklace.
Colour the right number of jewels on that necklace in the same colour as the number box.

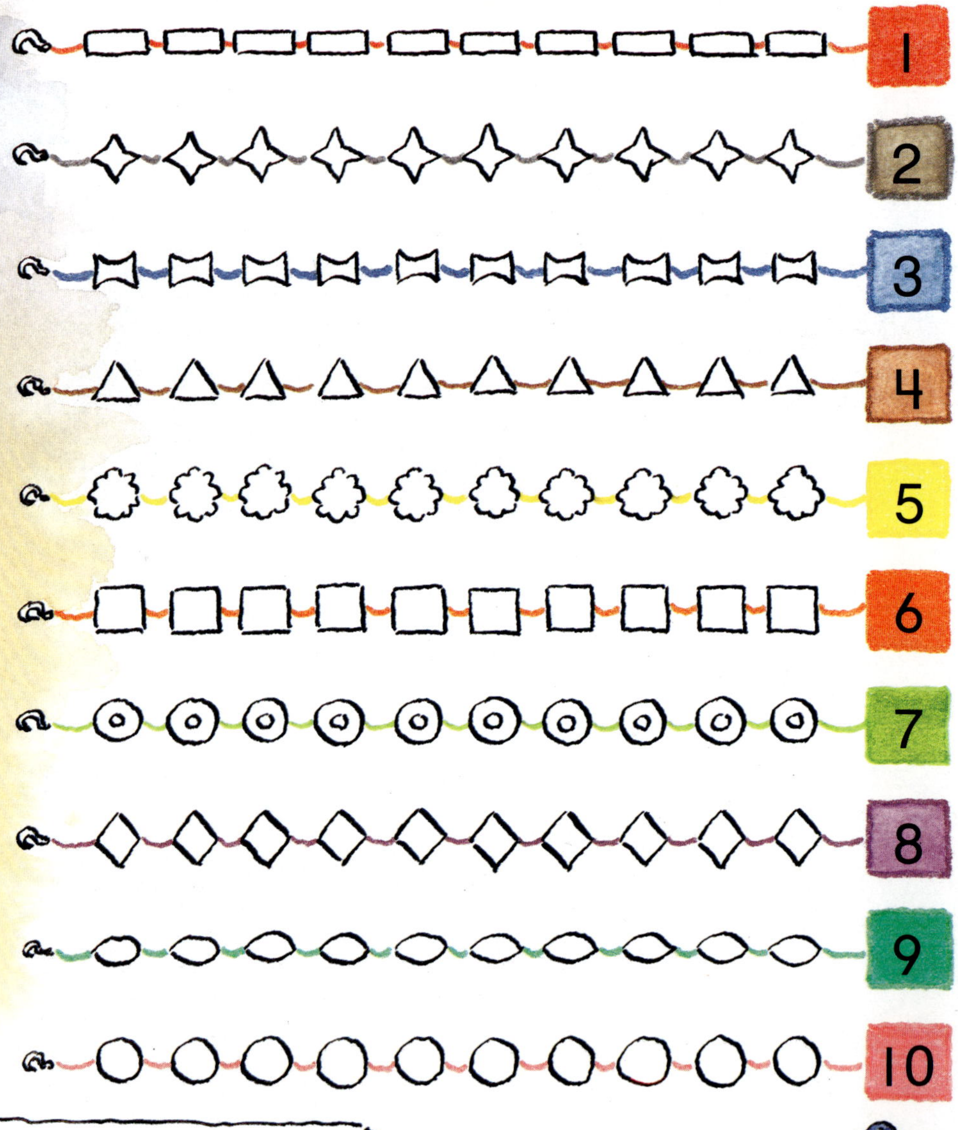

# Dotty castle

# Toy shop

Choose 6 toys and say the sound which the word starts with.

Ask someone to help you write the names here.

# Writing

Trace over these patterns starting at the ➤.

o o o o o o

c c c c c c

a a a a a a

d d d d d d

g g g g g g

q q q q q q

# Reading together

William got a big  for his birthday. Inside was a  set. It had a 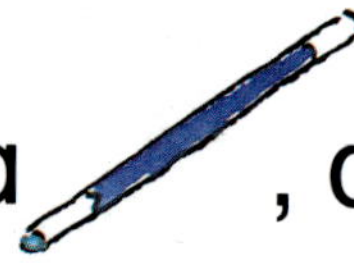, a  and a . There was also a  of spells. He pointed the  at the  and it turned into a . Just then Dad came in and William pointed the  at him. He turned into a ...............

flower parcel cloak magic
magic wand book cat top hat

Choose from these words to complete the story.

# Feelings

Talk about the things which make you feel happy, sad, angry or frightened. Ask someone to help you make these lists.

happy

sad

angry

frightened

# Spellings

Look at the pictures below. Say each word aloud and then fill in the missing letter sound from those shown.

h p f m b c d r

_ op

_ at

_ ed

_ og

_ at

_ ig

_ ox

_ ug

n m g l s p x t

ow _

ju _

pi _

ba _

bu _

cu _

ja _

bo _

# A word think tank

Write as many words as you can think of that tell us about water. How does it feel? What does it do? Write one in each splash.

# Right word

Draw a line under the correct word.

The little boy is standing on the platform/ steps/ chair.

The mother is looking in her bag/ pocket/ coat.

The guard is waving a flag/ cup/ hat.

The engine at this platform is blue/ green/ red.

# Dinosaur world

Make your own dinosaur world. You will need:

•glass or plastic bowl •cling film •plants with roots
•old spoon fixed to a stick to use as a spade
•gravel •compost •rocks •small models

What to do:

I Put gravel into the bottom.

2 Add a layer of compost.

3 Position plants and rocks.

4 Water.

5 Put in figures.

6 Cover the top with cling film.

Your garden will not need watering for many weeks. Watch how it 'rains' inside.

# Build a car

Use Lego, Duplo or Stickle bricks to build a car that will carry a small doll or a heavy load like a metal toy.

Think about:

**1** The chassis (base)... Will it be like this?

**2** How many wheels are needed?

**3** How will they be fixed to the chassis?

**4** The carrying space.

**5** How will it look when it is finished?

# A kaleidoscope

Make this amazing toy.

You will need:

- scissors • sticky tape • glue
- card (9 cm long and 9 cm wide)
- kitchen foil or silver paper • colourful bits and pieces

What to do:

1 Glue the foil to the card and smooth it out.

2 Cut the card carefully into 3 equal pieces.

3 Tape the 3 pieces together as shown.

4 Look down the tube at small colourful objects.

What can you see if you look at one object or at several? How many reflections can you see?

# Shadows

Place a lamp so that the shadow of an object is cast on the wall.

The lamp is like the sun. If a solid object is in the path of the light then the light can't pass through and a shadow is cast behind it.

Shine a light through something transparent.
What happens? You can use a torch.

What sort of shadow do these things make?

- hand
- glass
- book
- balloon
- pencil
- shoe

What made these shadows? Match them with the objects below.

**shadows**

**objects**

pencil hand matchbox book hands

# Home from school

This is a game for two or three players.
How to play:

- Start at school, use a dice and take turns.
- If you land on a picture square you get help.
- If you land on a danger flash ✷ you get a forfeit.
- The first player home is the winner.

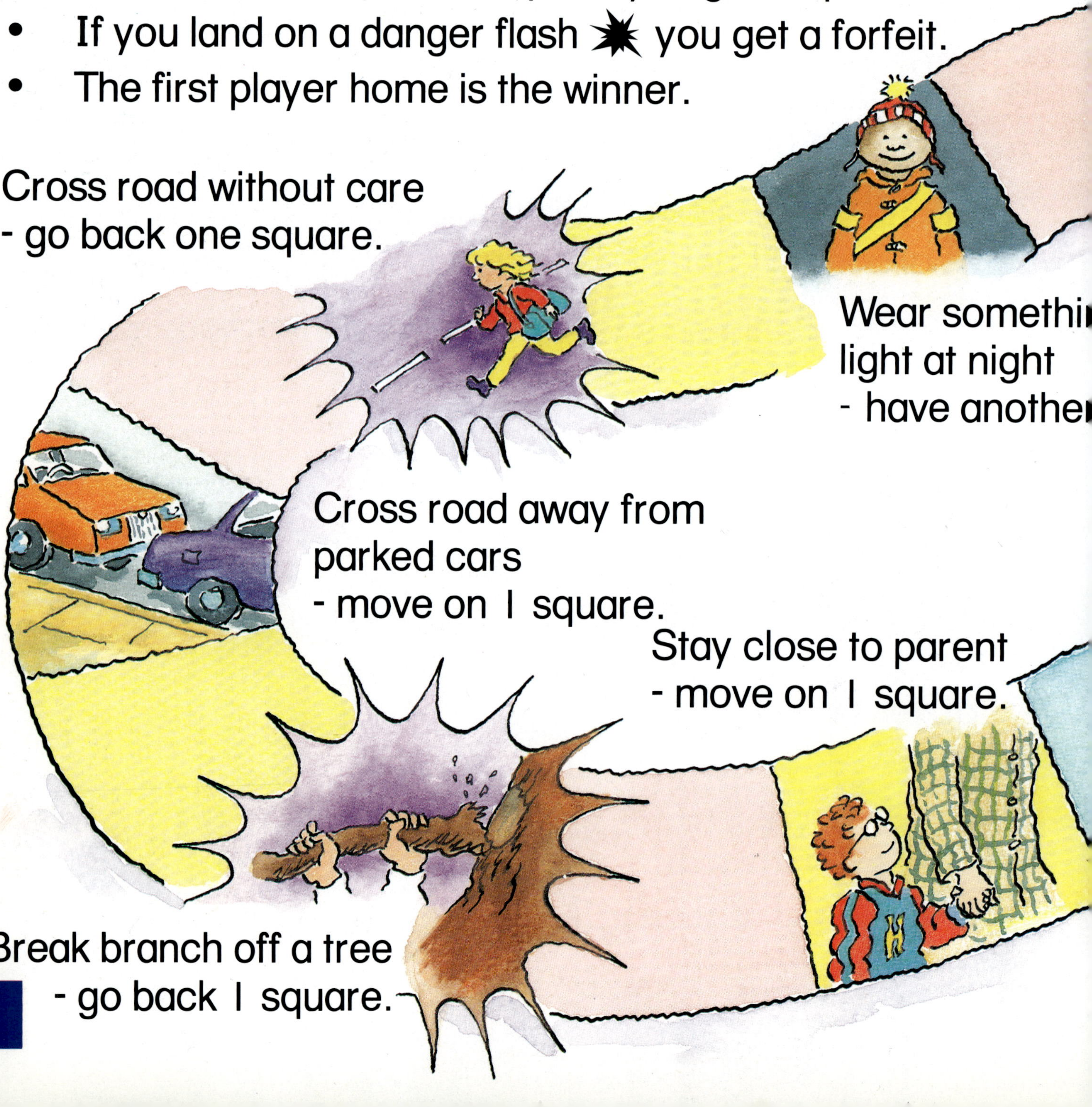

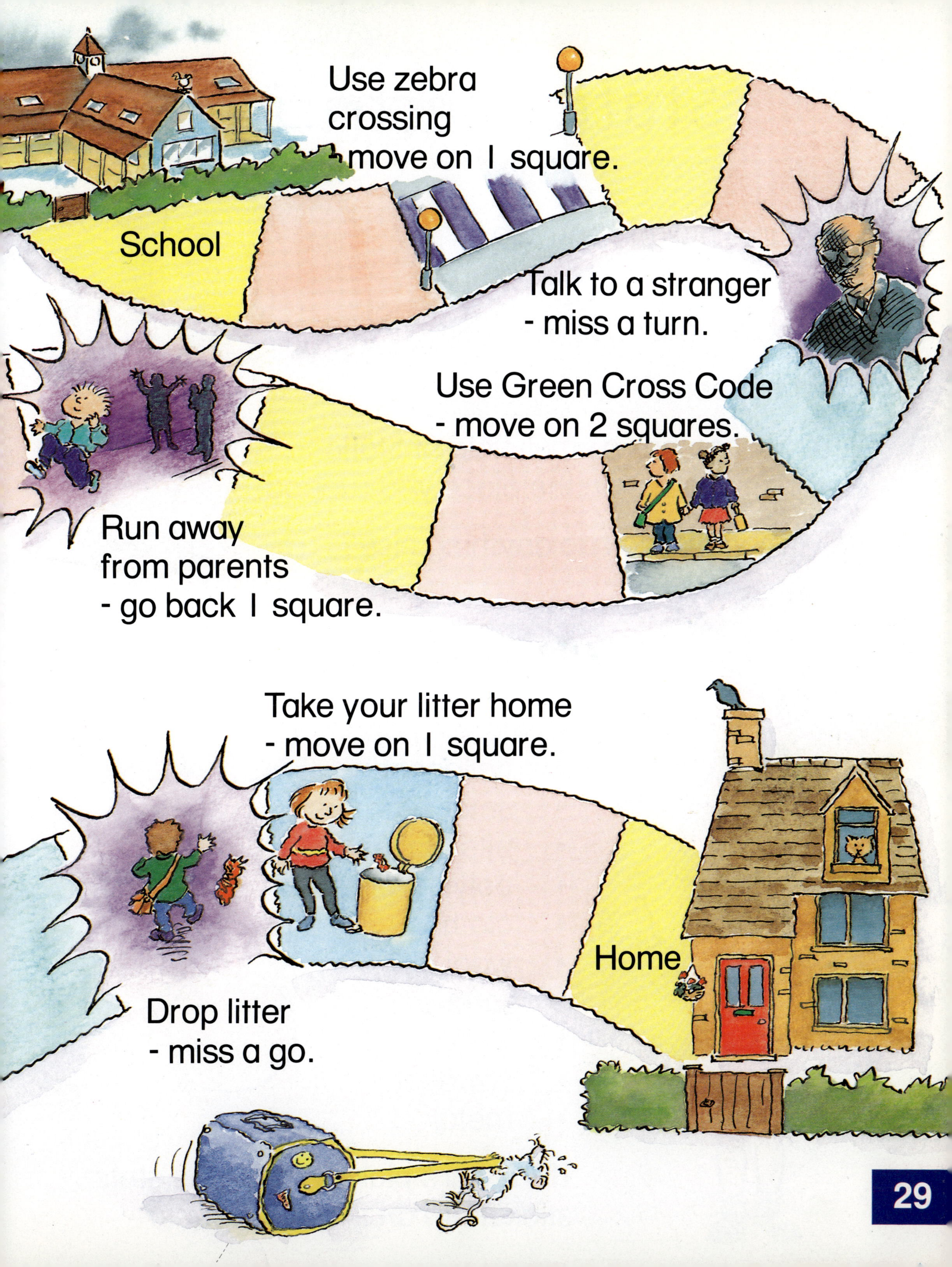
School
Use zebra crossing - move on 1 square.
Talk to a stranger - miss a turn.
Use Green Cross Code - move on 2 squares.
Run away from parents - go back 1 square.
Take your litter home - move on 1 square.
Drop litter - miss a go.
Home

# Static electricity

Blow up a balloon and rub it on your hair or on your jumper.

Now hold it near someone else's hair!

What happens?

Your balloon has a small field of static electricity near it, in the place you rubbed.

Will this static pick up anything else?

Now try picking up tiny bits of the following:

- tissue paper
- cellophane
- small feathers
- bits of plastic
- polystyrene
- cloth
- wool
- food
- wood
- sawdust
- metal

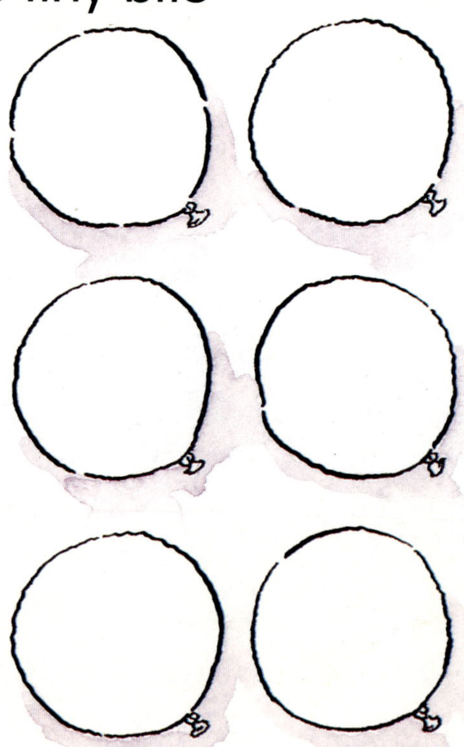

If they are picked up by the static, stick them on these balloons.

# All about me

Name ______________________

Age ______________________

Boy or girl ______________________

This is me →

I was born in ______________________

Height ______________________

Weight ______________________

Colour of hair ______________________

Colour of eyes ______________________

Shoe size ______________________

Names of brothers and sisters ______________________

______________________

Mum’s name ______________________

Dad’s name ______________________

Other facts ______________________

# HEADStart

## A complete home-learning range.

When your child has completed this book, there are plenty of others to choose from the Headstart range.

Here is a selection:

**Your Child at ...**
Each of these books practises skills in English, Maths and Science.
- Your Child at 4
- Your Child at 5
- Your Child at 6
- Your Child at 7

**Headstart 3-5**
Each book practises skills which will prepare children for their first years at school.
- Read & Write
- Counting
- Shape & Colour
- Science

**Headstart Early Skills**
Activities help children to learn to tell the time and use a calculator.
- Tiger Time
- Calculator Alligator

**Headstart 5-7**
National Curriculum skills practice for children at Key Stage 1.
- Handwriting
- Reading & Writing
- Spelling
- Number
- Measuring & Shape
- Science

British Library Cataloguing in Publication Data
Whiteford, Rhona
Your Child at 5
I. Title II. Fitzsimmons, Jim
649

ISBN 0-340-59097-1

First published 1993
Impression number 10 9 8 7 6 5 4 3 2 1
Year 1998 1997 1996 1995 1994 1993



Printed in Hong Kong for the educational publishing division of Hodder & Stoughton Ltd, Mill Road, Dunton Green, Sevenoaks, Kent TN13 2YA by Colorcraft.

Photography: Roddy Paine, Tunbridge Wells.
The children in the photographs are wearing clothes in the Ladybird range, produced exclusively for Woolworths plc and available in selected stores.